EIGHT BEST

FEIJOA RECIPES

*Easy and delicious ways to deal
with the glut of feijoas in April*

Kwizzel Publishing
86A Lynn Road
Bayview
Auckland 0629 New Zealand
kwizzelnewzealand@gmail.com

Cover: the author's photo of feijoas from her garden.

ISBN 978-0-473-32438-4

Contents   Page

My notes:

An introduction

Feijoa, a favourite fruit which thrives in warmer parts of New Zealand and in South America, is a variety of guava. During April trees are laden and for about three weeks everyone is flush with feijoas. There seem to be bucketfuls available in every neighbourhood.

All these recipes would work equally well using yellow guavas. When you cut a yellow guava you'll see it is similar to a feijoa. Cherry or red guavas aren't the same.

I have used as a reference for size an average home garden feijoa in these recipes. That is a little larger than a number 7 egg, or about 7 cm long unpeeled. A similar yellow guava would nestle in the palm of a woman's hand.

A moderate sized coffee mug will be useful as a measuring cup. Three and a half mugs of wet or dry mixture should fill a litre bottle.

All spoon measurements are for a level spoonful unless otherwise stated.

Here's a really easy recipe to start you off.

Poached feijoas and custard

You can use this recipe with cornflakes or muesli for breakfast; and forget the custard. You'll need ripe but not over-ripe fruit for this recipe.

Peel and slice 6 feijoas.
Place in a shallow pan and just cover with water. Simmer till softened.
Add 2 rounded tablespoons sugar and juice of 1/2 lemon. Stir gently until the sugar is dissolved. Cover the pan and allow to come back to the simmer stage and leave another 2 minutes.

You may want to scoop the fruit out with a slotted spoon; any remaining juice is great to cook in your morning porridge.

The poached feijoas will keep well in the fridge for 3 days.

Handy hint: as you slice each feijoa for this recipe drop them into boiling water immediately to save them going brown.

Your own home made custard

Mix two dessertspoons of custard powder and 1 1/4 dessertspoons of sugar in a small bowl suitable for microwaving. Gradually stir in 2 cups of milk. You can use full cream milk, the blue top or calcium enriched milk. If you only have trim milk in your fridge you'll get a better result by whisking in a dessertspoon of full cream milk powder during the first pause in microwaving.

Cook on microwave high for 2 1/2 – 3 minutes, stopping four or five times during the process to stir the custard. Keep a watch out, and when the mixture rises in the jug/bowl stop cooking immediately. Once out of the microwave give the mixture a final stir, then cover loosely with cling film and press it close to the custard which prevents a skin forming when it has cooled. This is quote a light custard and delicious with many desserts.

If you want a thicker or sweeter custard adjust the amount of custard powder and sugar. An extra 1/2 dessertspoon of each will be enough. Note: Edmonds Custard powder is gluten free.

Feijoa and apple crumble

The fruit:
8 – 10 feijoas
2 apples, preferably granny smith
2 dessertspoons white sugar
juice of half a lemon

The crumble:
4 tablespoons white flour
6 tablespoons rolled oats
2 tablespoons desiccated coconut
3 tablespoons brown sugar
2 1/2 tablespoons butter or spread

Peel and slice the feijoas, peel core and slice the apples so that the pieces are about the same as the feijoa slices. Gently poach the apples and feijoas together till the apples are soft, add the sugar and lemon juice and stir through while still on the heat until the sugar has dissolved. Put this mixture into a shallow baking dish of about 4 cups capacity.

While that mixture is cooking, prepare the crumble mixture. You'll need to soften the butter, and then push it through the flour with a fork before adding the other dry ingredients. When all the crumble ingredients have been mixed together spoon them lightly over the cooked fruit.

Bake in a moderate oven for 12 - 15 minutes so that the crumble cooks through, and if necessary grill at the very last so that the top is nicely browned.

Custard from the poached feijoa recipe is ideal with this dessert, with a good scoop of vanilla ice cream on the side.

Feijoa and apple muffins

My tip when making muffins: you may use a mini bench top oven, and most recommend baking only six muffins at a time. That is still economical in power usage because the little oven heats very quickly. I have given up using flexible pans as the muffins often don't cook through properly. When I'm using a standard metal muffin pan I line it with paper muffin cases as it is so much easier to clean afterwards. I spray the pans and the paper cups first. It's easier to peel the paper off the muffin if you have done this. These muffins aren't too heavily loaded with extra sugar as the fruit has its own natural sweetness.

I prefer to use standard or plain flour for all my baking and add the baking powder. You know you have the freshest mix this way. I know olive oil is very good for our health, but it's too heavy and strongly flavoured to use in baking. I prefer sunflower or safflower oils.

Gently mix the following ingredients together with a fork:

3/4 cup white flour
3/4 cup wholemeal flour
3 teaspoons baking powder *(If using self raising flour halve the amount of baking powder)*
2 rounded tablespoons brown sugar or raw sugar
2/3 teaspoon ground ginger

Add:
1/2 large apple, grated
        Use a crisp apple such as Braeburn.
the finely chopped flesh of 3 feijoas
                        (see the hint #2 on page 13)

In a separate small bowl whisk an egg
with 1 1/2 tablespoons of canola oil
                (or some other light cooking oil)
add 1/2 cup of milk

Stir this wet mixture lightly through the dry mixture. Do this gently till all the flour has been moistened, but not any longer. If you need a little extra milk to make the mix moist enough drizzle it in slowly. The amount of milk needed varies according to the brand of flour you're using, and the moisture in the feijoas.

Use a large fork to stir the dry ingredients together and a tablespoon to gently turn the wet mixture through the dry. Don't use an electric food mixer or the mixture will be too wet.

Have 6 to 8 muffin cups greased with baking spray, and gently fill each muffin cup no more than 2/3rd full. Bake for 12 to 15 minutes at 180° C.

Muffins are best eaten the same day, and any left-overs will keep well in your freezer.

Feijoa and blue cheese muffins

This is gourmet stuff. The feijoa sweetness is nicely set off by the tang of blue cheese.

3 feijoas

1/2 cup white flour
3/4 cup wholemeal flour
2 1/2 teaspoons baking powder.
1 dessertspoon sugar

75 gm blue vein cheese
1 1/2 tablespoons good quality cooking oil.
(Safflower or sunflower oils are good)
1 egg
1/3 cup of milk

Peel and cut the feijoas into tiny pieces.

Spray paper muffin cases with oil; and stand in muffin or patty tins. It's a good idea to do this so that the paper cases don't collapse, but you won't have to spend ages cleaning the muffin tray.

Stir the flour, baking powder and sugar together with a fork. In a separate bowl whisk the egg, add the oil and whisk them together. Then add all the other ingredients including the feijoas. It's best that they're added raw or they'll be too wet for the mixture.

Scoop large spoonfuls into the prepared muffin cases.
Bake at 180° – 200° C. You may have to experiment with the first batch until you get to know your oven's idiosyncrasies.

Makes 6 – 8 depending on the size of your muffin pans. Eat warm and enjoy!

Handy hints:
#1: Again, about the use of plain or self raising flour. The usual proportion for most muffin recipes is 2 teaspoons of baking powder to one cup of flour. You'll need just half that amount of baking powder if you're using self raising flour.

#2: Peel your feijoas, then cut them in half. Scoop out most of the wet inside and discard *or keep for jam*, and then cut the ring of flesh into smaller pieces. Using only the flesh of the fruit instead of the soft middle in this recipe will prevent the muffins being too sticky when cut.

#3: If using a bench top mini oven, start the muffins on the middle rack for 10 minutes, and then move to the top rack for last 5 to 6 minutes. Total cooking time at 180° will depend on the power of your particular oven. My oven instructions are to bake only 6 at a time.

Feijoa cake

12 feijoas
1/3 cup canola oil (*or other light cooking oil*)
1 heaped tablespoon of good brand canola spread
3 x #6 eggs,
        (*or 2 x #7 eggs + the yolk of one #7 egg*)
3/4 cup raw or brown sugar

1 cup white flour
1 1/4 cups wholemeal flour
2 teaspoons baking powder
1/2 teaspoon baking soda
1/2 teaspoon cinnamon
1/2 teaspoon mixed spice

Peel the feijoas and mash them with the canola oil, or put all in a blender.

Soften the canola spread and whisk the eggs with it. Dissolve the sugar in the egg mixture, then add the feijoas and canola oil.

Mix all the other ingredients then: gently pour most of the wet mixture into the dry, lifting the mixture from the edges of the bowl into the middle. Save a little of the wet mixture and add at the end if you need it for the right cake consistency. It should be a slightly wet mixture, but not runny.

Line a 21 cm round cake tin with greaseproof/lunch paper or baking paper. Rub some canola spread across the paper and any sides of the tin not covered with paper. A round tin ensures more even baking.

Pile the cake mixture gently into the prepared tin and cook at 160° C for 35 - 40 minutes.

Test that the cake is cooked right through. The easiest way to do this is to slip a sharp knife blade into the cake and see if it comes out clean. Leave the cake in the tin for 15 minutes before turning out onto a wire rack to cool. Don't remove the paper till the cake has cooled.

The finished product may have a slightly crisp top. This is because of the water in the feijoas. It's not a calamity if that happens, it'll still taste great. This cake has a good texture throughout, but if the crisp top bothers you it is soon softened with a cream cheese icing, or a colourful icing for the kids.

Preserves

Feijoa chutney with acknowledgement to the master, Digby Law

1 kg feijoas,
200 gm onions
200 gm pitted dates
350 gm brown sugar
1 tablespoon ground ginger
1/2 teasp ground cloves
2 teasp salt
3 1/2 to 4 cups vinegar

Soften the dates by soaking in just enough hot water to cover them; leave for one hour.
Peel the feijoas and cut into small pieces.

Cut the onions into small rings and then once or twice across. Combine all the ingredients in a large heavy bottomed saucepan or pot. Bring to the boil and cook very gently for at least 40 minutes. Keep stirring gently and ensure that the mixture doesn't stick to the bottom of the pan.
Many people will cook this for up to an hour and a half. I watch my power bill and stop cooking somewhat sooner than many do. Your chutney should thicken. Pour into hot sterilised jars and seal.
Makes about 8 medium sized jars of delicious chutney.
Leave for at least 2 weeks before using so the flavours can meld together.

Handy hints.
#1: I prefer to use either white vinegar or cider vinegar in all the recipes calling for vinegar as it is more easily tolerated by those with gastric/intestinal problems.

#2: See Hint #2 on page 22 about sterilising the jars.

Pickled feijoas; an unusual adaptation
of cucumber bread and butter pickles.

18 good sized feijoas
1 medium sized onion

Preparing the fruit:
3 litres cold water
1 tablespoon salt

The pickling liquid:
1 litre white vinegar
1 3/4 cups white sugar
2 teaspoons plain salt
1 dessertspoon peppercorns
1 large whole chilli, or three smaller ones

Peel the feijoas, and drop them in the cold salted water for one hour.

While you're waiting, sterilise sufficient glass jars in which to put the sliced feijoas.

Slice the onion finely and chop the chillis on a wooden chopping board.
Put the vinegar, sugar, onion and all other pickling ingredients into a pot and bring to the boil. Simmer for 5 minutes.

Slice each feijoa 2 - 3 mm in thickness across the diameter so that a wheel pattern shows.

After 5 minutes drop the sliced feijoas into the simmering pickling liquid and keep on the stove for another three minutes.

Using a non-metallic slotted spoon scoop the fruit into the sterilised jars. Then fill with the pickling liquid, and seal. If you're using metal lids cover the jar with a layer of cling film first to prevent the vinegar reacting with the metal.
Makes 5 – 6 jars, jam jar size.

Handy hints.
#1: After peeling each feijoa, and before slicing the lot, drop them into a pot of cold salted water. Use one tablespoon of salt to 3 litres of water. This will prevent them turning brown too quickly and also begin the pickling process.

#2: After chopping the chillis be sure to wash your hands well before putting your hands near your face. Don't use the same chopping board for cutting up pet food unless you've scrubbed it well.

#3: Simmering means having the heat set so that the liquid just keeps moving as tiny bubbles come to the surface. Don't leave the lid on the pot once it has reached simmer temperature.

Feijoa jam

This jam doesn't have the sweet cloying flavour you might expect because of the hint of ginger.

1/2 bucket of ripe feijoas
1 cup water
sugar *(measured at the second stage)*
1 dessertspoon powdered ginger, or a tablespoon of grated fresh ginger

You will have gathered the fruit and allowed it to ripen over a few days. Have a large casserole sort of pot that can be used on the stove top element.

When they're ripe, peel the feijoas and chop into small pieces. They don't have to be even shapes, just small enough so they'll mush up in the eventual jam mixture. If you have a lot of fruit you may prefer to cut them in half and scoop out the flesh.

Put the water in the saucepan, and then add the chopped feijoas. Gently bring to the boil, stirring with a wooden spoon now and again. Once boiling, keep on a rolling boil till the fruit softens. Set aside to cool.

Measure your fruit and its juice. Put the fruit into the cleaned saucepan. Measure exactly the same amount of sugar and add to the fruit mixture. Stir the sugar in well, add the ginger and then place the saucepan on the stove again.

Now you're going to need to be more vigilant with your stirring as it heats or the sugar may burn.

Heat the jam mixture stirring all the while, and let it boil for at least ten minutes. You'll need to test for the right jam consistency, and boil still further if necessary until it's right. Stir in any foam that's rising to the top.

You can test if the jam is ready to take off the heat by dropping about 1/2 teaspoonful, or less, onto a cold saucer. If a skin forms on this droplet you're right for bottling the jam in sterilised jars.

Handy hint #1: It's far preferable to use a wooden spoon as that slides across the bottom of the pan when you're stirring and saves the mixture from sticking and burning. Hold this spoon level when you take it out of the boiling mixture. When the dribble left on the spoon hangs there and doesn't fall then the jam's ready.

I have a friend who thought she should boil the fruit and sugar mixture till this hot mix was as thick as the jam she wanted. She ended up with fruit toffee. The mixture had been boiling too long.

(there are further bottling hints over the page)

#2: The easiest way to measure a large quantity of cooked fruit is to use a one litre measuring jug. Make sure you've rinsed the jug with boiling water, and especially if you're pouring from this into the jars when the jam is cooked.

#3: Sterilising the jars: I find the easiest way is to put a little water into very clean jars and microwave them. About 45 seconds for one jar is quite enough, and adjust that for three at a time to 1 minute 30 seconds. After removing the jars from the microwave, and emptying out the water, put a long handled spoon into each jar before you pour the hot liquid in. This helps avoid the glass cracking as the spoon will absorb the shock of sudden change in temperature. I do exactly the same if I am pouring a cold mixture into a hot jar.

Many cooks prefer to use the standard method of heating the jars in an oven set at 50°.

#4: If your jam is somewhat runny after bottling that's better than too thick. Leave the covered jars in sunlight or another warm place and in a day or two they will thicken satisfactorily. Leaving them in the fridge without covering will also do the trick.

All the recipes in this book have been tested in a
home kitchen by an experienced cook.

About the author:

When June Allen moved into her present home in Bayview, Auckland, N.Z. she found an old feijoa tree in her yard. This tree produces magnificent fruit year after year, and June's neighbours and friends enjoy helping her eat them.

When she's not cooking, gardening or having coffee with friends, June Allen is writing fanciful stories for young children. They're delightful books which feature New Zealand creatures.

Like us on Facebook: Kwizzel Publishing